YOU ARE ENOUGH

Thirty Mini Mantras for Self-Transformation
Be Empowered, Enlightened, and Inspired

By Author and Artist Zoe Summer

"I believe that simple is the new brilliant, and Zoe Summer
is masterful at getting right to the core of your heart
in ways that only take a few minutes per day."
—Tiamo De Vettori

YOU ARE ENOUGH
By Author and Artist Zoe Summer
Foreword by Tiamo De Vettori

Balboa Press books may be ordered through booksellers or by contacting:

Balboa Press
A Division of Hay House
1663 Liberty Drive
Bloomington, IN 47403
www.balboapress.com
1 (877) 407-4847

ISBN: 978-1-5043-3776-2 (sc)

Library of Congress Control Number: 2015912058

Printed by RRD China.

Balboa Press rev. date: 10/29/2015

BALBOA
PRESS
A DIVISION OF HAY HOUSE

To all whom this book may Serve. It is my hope that it will bring you inner peace to know that all your answers are within each of you, and that we are all "One."

If the only prayer you ever say in your entire
life is thank you, it will be enough.
—Meister Eckhart

CONTENTS

One-Minute Miracles For Busy People:

♥

Mini Mantras And Flower Mandalas

FOREWORD

In search of meaning, purpose, and transformation, some people climb to the top of the world's highest summits, some get their PhD, some attend ten-day meditation retreats, and some write their first book. While these are all tremendous accomplishments, perhaps the tipping point to the life you truly desire can be found in ways that take far less time, effort, and perseverance.

On my path to purpose and success, I've learned firsthand that to achieve, you have to believe—especially in your darkest hours when you may be filled with doubt, fear, and insecurity. When you feel broken, you have to break through. When you get turned down, you have to turn it up. When people react in fear, you respond in grace. To reach that level of inspiration, trust, and peace, it comes down to one thing: unconditional self-love. So how do we get there?

What I love most about Zoe Summer's book, *YOU ARE ENOUGH,* is that she provides a very practical, easy way for you to begin your journey back to self-love. I believe that simple is the new brilliant, and Zoe Summer is masterful at getting right to the core of your heart in ways that only take a few minutes per day.

To reach ultimate self-love, you have to recondition your subconscious belief system about the Truth of who you really are—which is infinite love, peace, wisdom, and joy. By reciting Zoe's powerful Mini Mantras every day for sixty days, you will feel yourself moving out of your head (where fear lives) and into your heart (where love expands). When you make choices, decisions, and actions from love, your inner and outer worlds will coalesce into the extraordinary.

As Zoe guides you toward the emergence of your true Self, what I love most about her work is that she does this in a way that only the greatest writers, artists, and light-workers know how to do. Rather than trying to penetrate the intellect, she says so much more with fewer words. In fact, each of her Mini Mantras contains only three words that carry great wisdom and brilliance that awaken the soul.

Zoe Summer's words bring us Home. At the same time, you'll find that Zoe holistically creates an enriching visual experience as she weaves in beautiful pictures of flowers which she calls "Flower Mandalas" that deeply compliment and embellish each Mini Mantra. In essence, rather than simply being a passive reader, you will become an active participant while creating the life that you truly desire.

Most people just read books. This book delightfully goes beyond that as the reader is taken on a visceral walk that is free of obligation, guilt, time constraint, and even learning. Why learning? Because you don't have to learn what you already know. You just have to remember.

After reading *YOU ARE ENOUGH*, you will remember the depth of your Greatness, your Power, your Wisdom, your Strength, your Purpose, your Light, and all the Love that lives inside you once you truly know that You … Are … Enough!

Be love,
Tiamo De Vettori
Transformational Speaker/Singer/Songwriter
LA Music Awards' Singer/Songwriter of the Year
TiamoMusic.com
TiamoKeynoteConcerts.com

ABOUT THE ART

This entire book was photographed with my iPhone 5c! To my knowledge, I am the very first artist to use "Mobile Photography" to illustrate a published book; therefore, *YOU ARE ENOUGH* is one-of-a-kind—just like You!

I lovingly and intentionally created everything in this book, and the art is no exception. Each and every time I pressed the shutter release, I simultaneously emanated Divine Love into the art, the "Flower Mandalas." You could say I sealed each photograph with a kiss! I call this self-helping, empowering, inspirational art "HE**ART**" (Heart+Art=He**ART**)!

I chose this method of photography because I wanted my intensely illuminating personal experience of photographing the Flower Mandalas in this book to feel timeless, spontaneous, and intimate for you too. I felt this particular camera lens perfectly translated my vibrant and vividly colorful vision for this book onto the pages. All the Flower Mandalas were shot in natural daylight in California with minimal Photoshop.

Just looking at a flower sets alight a person's happiness—flower power! To expand upon that cheerfulness, I selected flowers with certain colors known to draw forth upbeat emotions. I also chose flowers with certain patterns of petals reflecting sacred geometry and intricate pathways that "unfold" to draw your gaze inward to You and the Universe within You.

Instead of exotic flowers such as orchids, I singled out flowers such as the daisy, since I want to share with you the uncommon beauty of so-called "common" flowers. Because my intention is that you too get to experience an awareness of the sacred in the ordinary—which is the realization that the ordinary is, in fact, extraordinary.

PREFACE

In these pages, I wanted to share with you how I see life. I see a miracle.

Although I wrote and took the photographs for this book, and my name is on the cover as author and artist, Source created this book through me. I can only take credit for showing up—and show up I did, fully.

ACKNOWLEDGEMENTS

This book is *everyone's* book. It was co-created from our joined Universal "Oneness." I am acknowledging and forever thanking with infinite gratitude for the continued blissful feeling of my Oneness connection to Source within me.

INTRODUCTION

A Spiritual Epiphany

I remember it so clearly:

Sobbing in the kitchen of my home that I had to leave, I asked aloud: "What do I have left?"

Immediately, I sensed a loving presence and heard these words:

"You have what you always had.
You have what is everything.
You have what you have always been.
You have what you will always be.
You are Love."

After that divine guidance, my self-love, which was previously absent, began to blossom. That transcendent experience taught me that the answer to "Who am I?" is the same for "Why am I here?" and "What is the purpose of existence and the meaning of life?"

Love.

You Are Enough

We tell ourselves, "I am not enough."

Your relationship to yourself affects your well-being, your vital abundance in all its manifestations—health, family and friends, emotional and physical intimacy, business, and money. Therefore, self-love is absolutely necessary. If you don't believe you are enough, lack of self-love will hinder your flourishing in every area of your life.

This book is an invitation to freedom. Although you are already "free" many people don't *feel* free. You can experience freedom by no longer being ruled by your emotions of self-restriction and outdated thoughts that do not serve you. You can do this through self-love and by connecting to Divine Love, which is Source, within you. Self-love is the unity of you and Divine Love, which is *Source* or *One*—"that" which you already are. You are All, and All is You.

By trusting the resulting natural process of transformation to unconditional self-love, your energetic vibration rises to higher levels, and you become open to receiving more and more of the infinite miraculous possibilities that are *you* as they unfold.

This book, *YOU ARE ENOUGH: Thirty Mini Mantras for Self-Transformation*, is a fun, easy, fresh and adventurous way to experience the joyous truth that you are enough and to simultaneously actualize your unconditional self-love. I created this book so you could love yourself unconditionally and fully accept and completely appreciate yourself *as you are now*, not based on any future conditions you think might need to happen in order for you to love yourself.

Please stop looking outside yourself, seeking for self-worth. The truth is, you are enough simply because you exist and are perfect without needing to do anything or be any specific type of person or fill any kind of role. It is time to see yourself through the eyes of love, and when you allow that love in, you set yourself free, recovering the natural state of freedom that is already yours.

Through this book you can learn how to overcome your suffering and emotional pain, in order to achieve Spiritual Transcendence to have a sustained blissful feeling in the modern world and feel exhilarated, elevated, and euphorically alive! This book offers you a kickstart to enlightenment.

The following pages contain text that I co-created with Source and call Mini Mantras. Our photographs I named Flower Mandalas. The Mini Mantras and Flower Mandalas and their placement as pairs in their particular order within this book inspire specific positive emotions in a certain progression, leading you to experience and build an everlasting foundation of self-love.

Mini Mantras are enlightening, positive, loving thoughts. They are similar to affirmations, but they are more spiritually powerful because they are three devotional words that when read silently, then spoken out loud in an "I AM [that]" reply and heard by you, take you deeper into your heart. The speed of this pathway is dramatically increased with contemplation of the Flower Mandalas.

The heart's path is the only path to enlightenment. When focused on the heart center of the Flower Mandala, your mind calms, and this simultaneously draws you into your own heart which is *your* spiritual center. This process centers you into the Now and connects you to *feel* the sustainable, blissful Oneness of Source within you.

It is then that you experience your natural state of Divine Love, limitlessness, freedom, inner peace, and joy. It is from this sacred space of Source energy that everything in your life is created, including your "earthly supplies." Miracles will occur naturally and you will experience high performance in all areas of your life. You can experience Spiritual Transcendence in the modern world we live in because you will be living your life from this highest level possible.

These duets are a sacred key to opening the portal to self-love—this portal is your heart, which is the center of life. All the power of life is within you, not outside you. You cannot get power from others; it is within you, and no one has the power to make your life better, as you might judge it, or bring you more love, except you. You create your own "happily ever after."

I call the Mini Mantra and Flower Mandala sets "One-Minute Miracles" because when using them as a tool in one minute of "clock-time," you can access transformation—a perfect tool for busy people!

Here is how to use the One-Minute Miracles: Read to yourself a Mini Mantra—for example, "YOU ARE ENOUGH"—while you focus deeply into the center of its partner Flower Mandala. Then say out loud in an "I AM [that]" reply: "I AM ENOUGH!"

This process creates your new loving beliefs by stating the Mini Mantra, acknowledging the thought, and then claiming that thought as a belief by echoing the words and declaring with loving emotion, "I AM [that]."

Repeating the Mini Mantras will reinforce their wisdom and truth to you. This method of unfolding awareness changes how you feel about yourself since beliefs are merely thoughts. Any thought can be changed and exchanged with a new thought, a new belief, which is what this book does. "I am not enough" is replaced with "I AM ENOUGH!" And soon thereafter, lack of self-love is replaced with self-love.

In using this one-minute technique, you will start to naturally breathe more deeply from your abdomen in a calm and relaxed manner and feel peaceful, whilst your energetic vibration level rises with uplifting feelings of joy, gratitude, limitlessness, and love.

Each Mini Mantra and Flower Mandala companion set complements one another as energetic transformers. To enhance this, extra white space surrounds each set on each page to visually stimulate a stillness of time to aid deep meditation and transformation. The sets elicit an allowing state of mind, which is the opposite of resistance, which primes you to be in the timeless Now in order to experience the present moment and become centered.

Through the technique of focusing so many of your senses onto reading and replying to the Mini Mantra while gazing into the center of the Flower Mandala, you shift to the inner space of the most powerfully deep connection that exists to you—Divine Love—which is Source. It is here, within, where you can always experience eternal love, inner peace, spiritual fulfillment, and nurturing.

As you meditate on the duets, they ignite the divine spark within you. This profound, spiritual transformation of awakening connects you with your essence—which is Divine Love, or Source. Love leads you home.

You might find fear arises within you as you read the loving words of a specific Mini Mantra if you don't yet believe its loving truth about yourself. Don't try to push away the fear. Otherwise, it will only resurface later. Instead, just casually notice it, and do not judge it. At the same time, keep repeating out loud the "I AM [that]" reply to that particular Mini Mantra while gazing into its Flower Mandala to release that fear, which will eventually fall away. You will feel a detachment from the fear, and it will not appear again.

Even if you read the entire book daily, that's less than an hour a day spent in a very important way—invested in you! Alternatively, you can meditate on one Mini Mantra for sixty consecutive days. Thus, you can either experience the book as a whole or the pages independently.

It takes thirty to sixty days to replace an old habit with a new one. Therefore, for optimal results, I recommend repeating the Mini Mantras daily for sixty days to replace your outdated, undesirable, and negative beliefs about yourself with new, desirable, and positive beliefs. This in turn will strengthen, support, and nurture feelings of self-esteem, self-trust, self-acceptance, self-respect, self-worth, self-confidence, self-fulfillment, and ultimately, unconditional self-love.

With the experiential wisdom that you are enough, worthy, and lovable, and that you are Divine Love, which is Source, your newfound, ever-flowing wellspring of self-love will cause your mind, body, heart, spirit, and soul to align. You are now fully living as *all* of you. You are empowered, and all your actions and experiences become heart-centered. You no longer try to hide your light. Your heart will sing, your spirit will soar, and you will feel free and truly alive!

Shine on!

One-Minute Miracles For Busy People:

Mini Mantras
And
Flower Mandalas

YOU ARE YOU

YOU ARE MIRACULOUS

YOU ARE HAPPY

YOU ARE GRATITUDE

YOU ARE JOY

YOU ARE BEAUTIFUL

YOU ARE ABUNDANCE

YOU ARE GIFTED

YOU ARE CONFIDENT

YOU ARE KIND

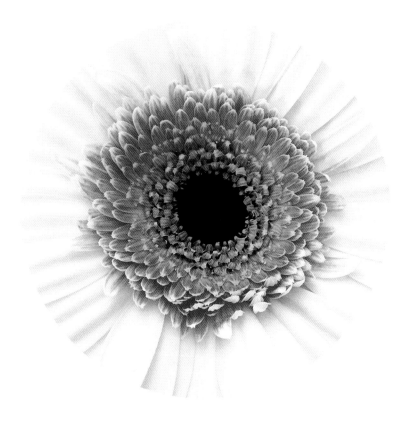

YOU ARE MAGIC

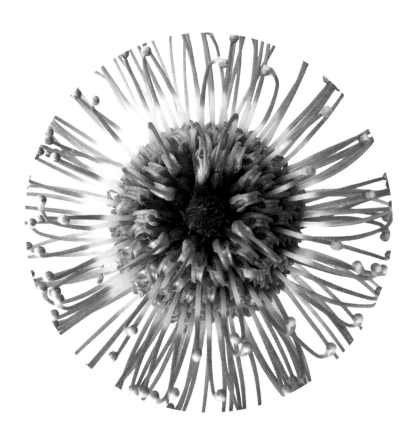

YOU ARE MAGNIFICENT

YOU ARE BALANCED

YOU ARE PASSION

YOU ARE CREATIVE

YOU ARE NOW

YOU ARE GENIUS

YOU ARE INFINITE

YOU ARE GRACE

YOU ARE COMPLETE

YOU ARE PEACE

YOU ARE FREE

YOU ARE ETERNAL

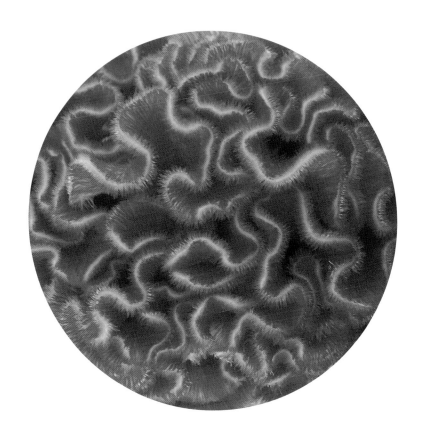

YOU ARE LIGHT

YOU ARE WORTHY

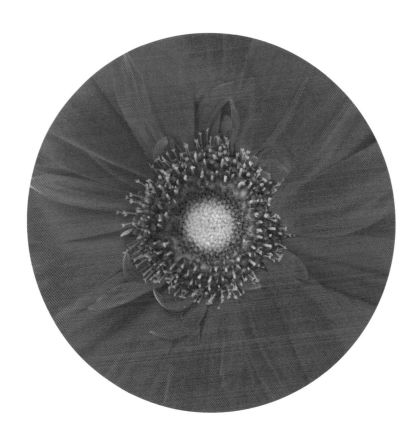

YOU ARE LOVE

YOU ARE POWER

YOU ARE ENOUGH

YOU ARE PERFECT

YOU ARE.